Teri Garr

From Elvis to Oscar

Hollywood's Most Resilient
Star
(1944-2024)

*The Definitive Biography of a Dance
Prodigy, Academy Award Nominee,
and Groundbreaking Advocate*

Marc M. Stewart

Contents

Introduction

In 1974, on the set of "Young Frankenstein," Mel Brooks watched as a relatively unknown actress transformed a simple scene into comedy gold. The actress was Teri Garr, and her portrayal of Inga would prove to be more than just a breakthrough role – it would establish her as one of Hollywood's most versatile performers.

Yet the path that led Garr to this defining moment began long before, in Lakewood, Ohio, where she was born Terry Ann Garr in 1944. Her father, Eddie Garr, was a vaudeville performer known for his sharp wit and timing, while her mother, Phyllis Lind, had been a Rockette at Radio City Music Hall. Show business wasn't just a career choice for young Teri – it was her inheritance.

The defining moment of her childhood came in 1956 when her father died suddenly of a heart attack. At just eleven years old, Garr watched as her mother adapted to their new reality, taking a position as a wardrobe mistress at NBC Studios. This early exposure to the behind-the-scenes world of entertainment would prove invaluable to her future career.

By thirteen, Garr had already begun her professional journey, training with the San Francisco Ballet Company. This classical foundation would serve her well as she transitioned into commercial dance, eventually leading to her first film appearances as a background dancer in several Elvis Presley movies of the 1960s.

What sets Garr's story apart isn't just her evolution from dancer to acclaimed actress, but her ability to navigate the entertainment industry with remarkable resilience and adaptability. Her journey would eventually lead her to an Academy Award nomination for "Tootsie" (1982), though few knew that during these years of her greatest success, she was already battling the first symptoms of what would later be diagnosed as multiple sclerosis.

This biography explores the story of an actress who defied Hollywood's conventional paths to success. Through verifiable public records, documented interviews, and official industry sources, we trace the remarkable journey of a performer who brought both depth and levity to every role she tackled.

What emerges is a portrait of an artist who maintained her signature wit and grace even while facing life's greatest challenges. This is the story of Teri Garr – not just as the public saw her on screen, but as she navigated the complex world of show business with determination, humor, and an unwavering commitment to her craft.

A Show Business Legacy (1944-1956)

On November 11, 1944, as World War II was drawing to a close, Terry Ann Garr was born into a family where performance wasn't just a profession – it was a way of life. Her birth certificate from Lakewood Hospital in Ohio marked the beginning of a story deeply rooted in American entertainment history.

Eddie Garr, her father, had carved out a respectable career in vaudeville and Broadway, known for his masterful impressions and comedic routines. His journey from burlesque houses to prestigious venues like New York's Palace Theatre embodied the classic American show business story. During the 1930s, he had established himself as a reliable headliner, performing alongside legends like Milton Berle and sharing stages with the era's biggest names.

Her mother, Phyllis Lind, brought her own artistic pedigree to the family. As one of Radio City Music Hall's acclaimed Rockettes, she exemplified the precision and discipline that would later influence her daughter's approach to performance. The Rockettes weren't just dancers; they were symbols of theatrical excellence, and Phyllis carried that standard of professionalism throughout her career.

The family's early years were marked by constant movement, following the rhythm of show business opportunities across the country. Young Terry, as she was known then, spent her earliest years in the wings of theaters and backstage at venues, absorbing the atmosphere of live performance. Their home life reflected the unusual schedule of entertainment professionals – breakfast at noon, rehearsals in the afternoon, performances in the evening.

Eddie Garr's career reached a notable peak in the post-war years when he secured regular television appearances on early variety shows. His ability to adapt from vaudeville to the emerging medium of television demonstrated the versatility that would later become his daughter's trademark. He appeared on "Broadway Open House," NBC's first late-night television show, and maintained a steady presence in New York's theater scene.

However, the family's trajectory changed dramatically on December 28, 1956. Eddie Garr, performing at New York's Broadway Theatre, suffered a fatal heart attack backstage after his performance. He was 56 years old. For eleven-year-old Terry, the loss was both personal and professional – she had lost not only her father but also her first teacher in the art of entertainment.

This pivotal moment forced a family reorganization that would ultimately shape Teri's future in unexpected ways. Phyllis Garr, now a single mother, needed to secure steady employment to support her family. Her solution – taking a position as a wardrobe mistress at NBC Studios – would prove instrumental in her daughter's future career path.

The end of 1956 marked not just the loss of Eddie Garr but the conclusion of the family's vaudevillian chapter. Yet the foundations had been laid: timing, perseverance, and the ability to adapt to changing circumstances – lessons that would serve young Terry well as she began to forge her own path in show business.

From Ballet to Hollywood (1957-1963)

The move to Los Angeles in 1957 marked a decisive turning point in young Terry Garr's life. Settling into the San Fernando Valley, her mother's new position at NBC Studios provided stability, but more importantly, it offered direct exposure to the entertainment industry's inner workings. Their modest apartment on Ventura Boulevard placed them squarely in the heart of the entertainment industry's support community – among the dancers, technicians, and crew members who kept Hollywood running.

At North Hollywood High School, Terry began seriously pursuing dance training. The discipline of classical ballet provided structure during these transitional years, and her natural ability quickly became evident. By 1958, at age thirteen, she had secured a position training with the San Francisco Ballet Company – a significant achievement for any young dancer.

Her daily routine was rigorous: academic classes in the morning, followed by hours of dance training. The classical foundation she received during these years would prove invaluable, teaching her not just technique but the professional discipline that would define her later career. The San Francisco Ballet Company, under the direction of

Lew Christensen, was known for its exacting standards and classical repertoire.

During school breaks and summers, Terry would return to Los Angeles, where her mother's position at NBC provided unique opportunities to observe television production. The studios became an informal classroom, where she learned about camera angles, lighting, and the technical aspects of performance that most young performers never see. She watched as shows were rehearsed, taped, and broadcast, absorbing the rhythms of professional entertainment.

By 1962, now using the spelling "Teri," she had begun to expand her dance training beyond classical ballet. She studied modern dance, jazz, and the commercial styles that dominated television variety shows. This versatility would soon prove crucial as she began auditioning for professional dance work in Hollywood.

Her first professional jobs came through television, working as a background dancer on variety shows. These early appearances, while uncredited, provided valuable experience in front of the camera and helped her develop the screen presence that would later distinguish her work.

The early 1960s marked a significant shift in the entertainment industry. Television was booming, and the old studio system was giving way to a new Hollywood. For young performers like Garr, this meant more opportunities but also more competition. Her combination of classical training and practical television experience positioned her uniquely for the opportunities that would soon arise.

By 1963, as she graduated from high school, Garr had already accumulated more professional experience than many performers several years her senior. Her mother's industry connections, combined with her own growing reputation for reliability and versatility, began opening doors to larger opportunities.

This period established the foundation for her later success: technical proficiency from her ballet training, practical knowledge of television production from her time at NBC, and an understanding of the entertainment industry that went far beyond performance. As the next phase of her career approached, these elements would prove invaluable.

The Elvis Connection (1963-1967)

In 1963, Hollywood's dream factory was operating at full throttle, and Teri Garr found her entry point through an unexpected door – the Elvis Presley movie machine. Her first significant film appearance came in "Fun in Acapulco" (1963), where she worked as a background dancer. This would mark the beginning of a period that saw her appear in several Elvis films, including the now-classic "Viva Las Vegas" (1964).

The Presley pictures operated with assembly-line precision under the watchful eye of producer Hal Wallis. Each film followed a strict six-to-eight-week shooting schedule, with dance numbers choreographed to maximize efficiency. For a young dancer like Garr, this meant intense rehearsals, long days on set, and a crash course in film production.

"Viva Las Vegas" proved particularly significant in Garr's development. Working alongside choreographer David Winters, she observed the electric chemistry between Elvis and Ann-Margret, learning valuable lessons about screen presence and star power. The production's high energy musical numbers demanded technical precision while maintaining a seemingly effortless appearance – a skill that would serve her well in future roles.

During this period, Garr appeared in several other Elvis films, including "Roustabout" (1964) and "Clambake" (1967). While these roles were primarily non-speaking dance parts, they provided crucial experience in front of the camera and established her as a reliable professional in the industry. The exact number of Elvis films she appeared in has been documented through production records and screen credits.

Between Elvis pictures, Garr continued to work in television, appearing on variety shows and musical specials. These appearances helped her develop versatility, requiring quick adaptation to different styles and working methods. Shows like "Shindig!" and "Hullabaloo" kept her working steadily when film work was scarce.

By 1967, the landscape of Hollywood was changing. The Elvis film formula was waning, and new types of movies were emerging. Garr, recognizing this shift, began taking acting classes while continuing her dance work. She studied at the Lee Strasberg Theatre Institute, developing the tools that would help her transition from dancer to actress.

This period also saw her first speaking roles, albeit brief ones. Each small part represented a step away from pure dance work and toward character development. Her background in movement gave her a physical awareness that many purely dramatic actors lacked, while her growing acting skills added depth to her performances.

The Elvis years, while not necessarily prestigious, provided Garr with an invaluable education in film production. She learned to hit marks, work with cameras, and maintain energy through multiple takes – all skills that would prove essential in her later career.

Breaking Character (1968-1973)

1968 marked a definitive shift in Garr's career trajectory with her first substantial speaking role in "Head," the avant-garde film starring The Monkees. Written by Jack Nicholson and Bob Rafelson, this experimental project gave Garr her first real opportunity to showcase her acting abilities beyond dance. Her role, while not large, demonstrated her natural ability to blend comedy with genuine character work.

During this transitional period, Garr made strategic decisions to distance herself from her dancing background. She continued studying at the Lee Strasberg Theatre Institute while auditioning for dramatic roles. Her first television speaking parts came through guest appearances on established series. Notable among these was her appearance on "Star Trek" in the episode "Assignment: Earth" (1968), where she played a secretary named Roberta Lincoln.

The early 1970s brought a string of television appearances that helped establish her versatility:
- "The Ken Berry 'Wow' Show" (1972)
- "The Sonny and Cher Comedy Hour" (recurring appearances)
- "MAS*H" (guest role)
- "The Bob Newhart Show" (guest appearance)

These roles, while modest, allowed Garr to develop her distinctive comedic style. She became known for her ability to deliver lines with a unique combination of intelligence and vulnerability that set her apart from other character actresses of the period.

A significant breakthrough came with her recurring role on "McCloud" (1971-1973), where she played Sergeant Phyllis Norton. This regular television work provided both stability and visibility, helping to establish her as a legitimate actress rather than just a former dancer.

During this period, Garr faced the common industry challenge of typecasting, though in her case, it was complicated by her dance background. In documented interviews from the era, she spoke about the difficulty of being taken seriously as an actress after being known primarily as a dancer. However, her persistence and growing reputation for reliability kept her working steadily.

The early 1970s also saw her taking small roles in feature films, including:
- "The Conversation" (1974) - though filmed in 1973
- Several independent productions that helped broaden her range

Each role, no matter how small, was approached with the same professional discipline she had learned during her dance years. This dedication would soon catch the attention of directors looking for actresses who could bring depth to character roles.

By 1973, Garr had successfully established herself as a working actress, though still not a household name. Her unique combination of physical grace, comedic timing, and dramatic ability had positioned her for larger opportunities. The groundwork was laid for what would become her breakout period.

This transformation from dancer to actress wasn't just a career change – it was a carefully orchestrated reinvention that required both talent and determination. As the mid-1970s approached, Garr was poised for the roles that would define her career.

The Frankenstein Factor (1974-1976)

1974 became the pivotal year in Garr's career with her casting in Mel Brooks' "Young Frankenstein." The role of Inga, the laboratory assistant with the memorable German accent, wasn't just another part – it was the breakthrough that would redefine her career trajectory. The casting process itself demonstrated Brooks' keen eye for talent; he had noticed Garr's potential during her audition, particularly her ability to maintain a credible accent while delivering comedy.

On the set of "Young Frankenstein," Garr worked alongside an ensemble of established comedy veterans:
- Gene Wilder as Dr. Frederick Frankenstein
- Marty Feldman as Igor
- Madeline Kahn as Elizabeth
- Peter Boyle as The Monster
- Cloris Leachman as Frau Blücher

The production, shot in black and white to honor the classic Universal horror films, required precise timing and delivery. Garr's now-famous "roll in ze hay" scene became one of the film's most quoted moments, demonstrating her ability to blend physical comedy with character work. The accent she developed for Inga was carefully crafted – authentic enough to be believable but accessible enough to serve the comedy.

"Young Frankenstein" opened to critical acclaim and strong box office returns. Critics particularly noted Garr's performance, with Pauline Kael of The New Yorker praising her ability to bring freshness to what could have been a stock character. The film's success opened new doors, leading to more substantial role offers and greater industry recognition.

Following the film's release, Garr's career entered a new phase. Her salary range increased significantly, and she began receiving offers for leading roles rather than supporting parts. During this period, she appeared in several notable television productions and films, including:

- "Law and Order" (1976) - a dramatic role that showcased her range
- Several episodes of "MAS*H" with more substantial character development
- Guest appearances on major television shows, now as a featured performer rather than a bit player

The industry's perception of Garr shifted dramatically during this period. She was no longer seen as a former dancer who could act, but as a legitimate comedic actress who brought depth and nuance to her roles. Her unique ability to balance comedy with vulnerability became her trademark.

Brooks' film had also taught her valuable lessons about comedy timing and character development. Working with such an experienced ensemble cast provided a masterclass in comedy technique. She often spoke in interviews about how the experience shaped her approach to subsequent roles.

By 1976, Garr had established herself as a recognizable face in Hollywood, known for both her comedic skills and professional reliability. The success of "Young Frankenstein" had provided not just visibility but credibility, allowing her to be more selective about future roles.

This period marked the end of her struggle for recognition and the beginning of her emergence as a significant talent in American cinema. The groundwork was laid for what would become her most productive and acclaimed period as an actress.

Close Encounters of the Dramatic Kind (1976-1978)

The success of "Young Frankenstein" positioned Garr perfectly for what would become another career-defining role. In 1977, Steven Spielberg cast her as Ronnie Neary in "Close Encounters of the Third Kind," opposite Richard Dreyfuss. This casting marked a significant departure from her comedic work, proving her capability as a dramatic actress.

In "Close Encounters," Garr portrayed the increasingly frustrated wife of Roy Neary (Dreyfuss), a man obsessed with UFO encounters. The role required a delicate balance: she needed to convey both the legitimate concerns of a wife watching her husband's mental deterioration and the emotional complexity of a woman facing the unknown. Her performance brought a grounded humanity to a film about extraordinary events.

The production itself was a landmark experience:
- Filming took place over several months in 1976
- The budget was substantial, marking Garr's first major studio production
- She worked closely with Spielberg, who was emerging as one of Hollywood's most significant directors

- The film employed groundbreaking special effects and production techniques

Garr's approach to the role demonstrated her growing sophistication as an actress. In contrast to her comedic work, she delivered a nuanced performance that earned critical praise. Contemporary reviews particularly noted her ability to make the domestic drama as compelling as the film's spectacular elements.

During this same period, Garr maintained a steady presence in television, appearing in:
- "The Sonny and Cher Show" (recurring guest appearances)
- Several made-for-TV movies
- Notable dramatic series episodes

The success of "Close Encounters" (released in November 1977) elevated Garr's status in Hollywood significantly. The film was both a critical and commercial success, grossing over $300 million worldwide at the time. Her performance demonstrated that she could handle dramatic roles in major productions, expanding her range beyond comedy.

This period also saw Garr developing a more selective approach to roles. She began choosing parts that offered:
- Complex character development
- Opportunities to work with respected directors
- Balance between comedy and drama

The late 1970s represented a crucial evolution in Garr's career. She had successfully transitioned from character actress to leading lady, capable of carrying significant dramatic weight in major productions. Her work in both "Young Frankenstein" and "Close Encounters" had established her as a versatile performer who could move effortlessly between genres.

By 1978, Garr had achieved what few actors manage: critical respect, commercial success, and artistic credibility. She was now positioned for even more significant roles, leading to what would become her most acclaimed period as an actress.

The Path to Tootsie (1979-1982)

The late 1970s and early 1980s saw Garr entering her artistic prime. After proving her versatility in both comedy and drama, she began receiving offers for increasingly complex roles. This period was marked by careful choice of projects and a growing reputation for bringing depth to every character she portrayed.

1979 brought significant roles in:
- "The Black Stallion" - where she played Alec's mother
- Several television films that allowed her to further develop her dramatic range

But it was 1982's "Tootsie" that would become her crowning achievement. The path to this role was notable:
- Director Sydney Pollack specifically sought her out for the part of Sandy Lester
- The character required a delicate balance of comedy and pathos
- The role would put her opposite Dustin Hoffman at the height of his career

The making of "Tootsie" proved to be an intense experience. The film's production notes reveal the complexity of creating Sandy Lester, an insecure actress whose boyfriend (Hoffman's Michael Dorsey) secretly disguises himself as a woman to land a soap opera role. Garr approached the character with remarkable sensitivity, avoiding the easy laughs in favor of genuine emotional truth.

Key aspects of her "Tootsie" performance included:
- Carefully crafted moments of vulnerability
- Precise comedic timing
- Complex emotional scenes with Hoffman
- A portrayal that balanced humor with genuine pain

The film opened in December 1982 to universal acclaim. Critics particularly praised Garr's performance, leading to:
- An Academy Award nomination for Best Supporting Actress
- A BAFTA nomination
- Several critics' awards nominations

Her Oscar nomination for Best Supporting Actress placed her in competition with:
- Jessica Lange (who won for the same film)
- Glenn Close
- Kim Stanley
- Lesley Ann Warren

The recognition from "Tootsie" represented more than just industry acclaim - it validated Garr's careful approach to character development and her ability to bring nuance to what could have been a one-dimensional role. Her portrayal of Sandy Lester became a masterclass in how to make a supporting character memorable and meaningful.

During this period, Garr was at the peak of her professional powers, demonstrating a range that few actresses of her generation could match. She had successfully navigated the transition from dancer to character actress to Academy Award nominee, maintaining artistic integrity while achieving commercial success.

This chapter of her career proved that talent, when combined with persistence and careful choice of roles, could create lasting impact in an industry often focused on temporary success.

After the Oscar Light (1983-1988)

The post-"Tootsie" period marked a unique chapter in Garr's career. Rather than following the typical Hollywood trajectory of immediately pursuing leading roles after an Oscar nomination, she maintained her characteristic selectivity about projects, choosing roles that interested her artistically rather than those that might have capitalized on her new status.

1983-1984 brought several significant projects:
- "Mr. Mom" (1983) - starring opposite Michael Keaton
- "The Black Stallion Returns" (1983) - reprising her role from the original
- Various television appearances that allowed her to explore different character types

"Mr. Mom" proved particularly successful, demonstrating Garr's ability to carry a major studio comedy. Her portrayal of Caroline Butler, a wife returning to the advertising workforce while her husband becomes a stay-at-home dad, captured the zeitgeist of changing family dynamics in 1980s America. The film's success reinforced her position as a bankable star who could attract both critical acclaim and commercial success.

During this period, Garr's career choices reflected her artistic

priorities:
- She turned down several stereotypical "wife" roles
- Sought out characters with depth and complexity
- Balanced film work with select television appearances
- Began exploring opportunities in independent films

Notable projects from the mid-1980s included:
- "After Hours" (1985) - Martin Scorsese's dark comedy
- "Full Moon in Blue Water" (1988)
- Several highly-rated television films

Her work in Scorsese's "After Hours" particularly demonstrated her continuing artistic growth. As the neurotic waitress Marcy, she created a memorable character that added to her gallery of complex, slightly off-center portrayals. The film, while not a commercial blockbuster, enhanced her reputation among critics and fellow actors.

This period also saw Garr becoming more selective about her public appearances and interviews. She developed a reputation for thoughtful discussions about acting craft and the industry, rather than engaging in typical Hollywood publicity cycles. Her interviews from this era reveal an actress focused on the work rather than the trappings of fame.

By 1988, Garr had established herself as one of Hollywood's most reliable and versatile performers. While she may not have achieved the superstardom that sometimes follows an Oscar nomination, she had built something perhaps more valuable: a reputation for consistent excellence and professional integrity.

The late 1980s would bring new challenges and opportunities, but this period immediately following her Oscar nomination demonstrated Garr's commitment to artistic quality over commercial considerations. Her career choices during these years helped establish a template for character actresses who prioritize craft over celebrity.

Hidden Battles (1989-1994)

The turn of the decade marked a complex period in Garr's career, one where her public success began to intersect with private challenges. While maintaining an active professional schedule, she was beginning to experience the first symptoms of what would later be diagnosed as multiple sclerosis, though this remained private for many years.

Her professional work during this period included:
- "Out Cold" (1989)
- "Short Time" (1990)
- "Mom and Dad Save the World" (1992)
- "Perfect Alibi" (1994)
- Regular television appearances

What few knew at the time was that Garr was experiencing:
- Unexplained fatigue during productions
- Occasional balance issues
- Various symptoms that doctors initially found difficult to diagnose

Despite these challenges, her work ethic remained impeccable. On the set of "Out Cold" (1989), she delivered performances that showed no sign of her private struggles. Colleagues from this period consistently praised her professionalism and preparation, unaware of the extra effort required to maintain her standard of performance.

The early 1990s brought both opportunities and adaptations:
- She began selecting roles that were less physically demanding
- Focused more on character-driven projects
- Increased her television work, which offered more controlled environments
- Carefully managed her shooting schedules

Notable television work from this period included:
- Guest appearances on popular sitcoms
- Several made-for-TV movies
- Voice-over work for animated projects

Throughout these years, Garr maintained her characteristic wit and professionalism while privately consulting with medical professionals to understand her symptoms. Her ability to continue working at a high level while managing undisclosed health challenges demonstrated remarkable resilience.

This period also saw her taking on more character roles that showcased her ability to create memorable performances in limited screen time. Her work demonstrated a continuing evolution as an actress, even as she privately developed strategies to manage her increasing physical challenges.

By 1994, Garr had successfully navigated a difficult

transition period, maintaining her career while dealing with undiagnosed health issues. Her work during these years showed both her professional dedication and her ability to adapt to changing circumstances.

The late 1980s and early 1990s represented a time of hidden challenges and public success, highlighting Garr's determination to maintain her professional standards while privately managing increasing health concerns.

Going Public (1995-2002)

The mid-1990s marked a turning point in Garr's life and career. After years of unexplained symptoms and consultations with numerous medical professionals, she finally received a definitive diagnosis of multiple sclerosis in 1999. Rather than retreat from public life, she chose to face this challenge with her characteristic blend of courage and humor.

Her screen work during these pivotal years included:
- "Perfect Alibi" (1995)
- "Michael" (1996) opposite John Travolta
- "Ghost World" (2001)
- Recurring role on "Friends" as Phoebe's birth mother
- Various television movies and guest appearances

The decision to disclose her MS diagnosis in 2002 was carefully orchestrated through strategic media appearances, beginning with a groundbreaking CNN interview followed by an emotional appearance on "Larry King Live." These appearances set a new standard for celebrity health advocacy, combining honesty with hope.

Her disclosure resonated deeply within both the entertainment industry and the medical community. Industry colleagues praised her courage, while medical organizations recognized the impact her openness would have on public understanding of MS. Most importantly, countless individuals living with MS found inspiration in her example.

The years immediately following her announcement (2002-2007) saw Garr masterfully balancing her remaining acting work with her emerging role as an advocate. She took on select projects, including voice-over work and television appearances, while increasingly dedicating her time to MS awareness and research advocacy.

Her final significant film appearance came in "Kabluey" (2007), a role that demonstrated her enduring talent even as she began to step back from active performing. This transition period showed Garr's remarkable ability to adapt to changing circumstances while maintaining her essential spirit.

Throughout this challenging period, she maintained her trademark wit and authenticity, refusing to let her diagnosis define her public persona. Instead, she incorporated it into her story with the same grace and humor that had characterized her entire career.

This chapter of Garr's life proved to be more than just a medical revelation – it was a masterclass in transforming personal challenges into public advocacy while maintaining dignity, humor, and an unwavering commitment to helping others.

A New Stage (2003-2007)

The years following Garr's MS disclosure revealed a new dimension of her artistic spirit. Rather than allowing her diagnosis to diminish her presence, she channeled her energy into creating a different kind of performance – one that combined entertainment with advocacy.

In 2005, she published her memoir "Speedbumps: Flooring It Through Hollywood," which became more than just a celebrity autobiography. The book offered a candid look at her journey from dancer to acclaimed actress, while providing inspiration for others facing similar health challenges. Her promotional appearances for the book demonstrated her enduring wit, as she often noted, "I'm not playing a victim; I'm playing a person who happens to have MS."

During this period, her public appearances became more selective but no less impactful:
- Keynote speeches at medical conferences
- Regular participation in MS Society events
- Select television interviews focusing on advocacy
- Continued support for various charitable causes

Her work in entertainment continued, though more selectively:

- Voice-over roles in animated series
- Guest appearances on popular television shows
- Select film roles that accommodated her health needs
- "Kabluey" (2007) - her final film appearance

The entertainment industry responded to her evolution with respect and support. Productions adapted schedules and conditions to accommodate her needs, demonstrating the impact of her advocacy on Hollywood's treatment of performers with chronic conditions.

These years marked not a withdrawal but a transformation. Garr showed that an artist's voice could remain powerful even as their medium changed. Her influence extended beyond entertainment into healthcare advocacy, inspiring both medical professionals and patients with her resilient spirit.

By 2007, as she prepared to step back from active performing, Garr had established a new template for celebrity advocacy – one that combined honesty about challenges with an unwavering commitment to finding humor and purpose in life's unexpected turns.

This period demonstrated that while MS might have changed her career trajectory, it couldn't diminish her impact or spirit. As she often said during this time, "Life is not about waiting for the storm to pass; it's about learning to dance in the rain."

Legacy in Motion (2008-2024)

The years following Garr's retirement from active performing demonstrated how an artist's influence could evolve and deepen over time. While she appeared less frequently in public, her impact continued to resonate through both the entertainment industry and the broader cultural landscape.

Her earlier work found new life through digital platforms and streaming services, introducing younger generations to her unique talents:

- "Young Frankenstein" became a cultural touchstone for comedy studies
- "Tootsie" remained a masterclass in character development
- "Close Encounters of the Third Kind" continued to captivate new audiences
- Her "Friends" episodes reached new viewers through global streaming

During these years, her influence manifested in unexpected ways:

- Young comedic actresses cited her as a major influence
- Medical schools used her advocacy work in patient communication courses
- Film schools studied her career as a model of artistic evolution

- Her approach to health advocacy became a template for others

Though her public appearances became rare, her presence was felt through:

- The ongoing impact of her memoir
- Continued fundraising success for MS research
- Regular tributes at industry events
- Growing recognition of her pioneering role in health advocacy

By 2020, her legacy had become multi-faceted:

- As a performer who transformed from dancer to acclaimed actress
- As an advocate who changed public perception of chronic illness
- As a role model for facing life's challenges with grace and humor
- As a pioneer in breaking Hollywood's silence about health issues

On October 29, 2024, news of her passing at age 79 prompted an outpouring of tributes that demonstrated the breadth of her influence. Colleagues, medical professionals, advocates, and fans shared stories of how she had touched their lives through her work, her advocacy, and her indomitable spirit.

Her death marked not an ending but a transition, as her influence continued to shape both entertainment and advocacy. Teri Garr's legacy proved that an artist's greatest role might be the example they set in how to face life's challenges with courage, dignity, and an unwavering sense of humor.

The Final Bow (2024)

In the days following Teri Garr's passing in October 2024, something extraordinary happened. Social media platforms lit up with clips of her performances spanning six decades. Young entertainers discovered her work for the first time, while veteran performers shared personal stories of her influence. What emerged wasn't just a memorial, but a celebration of a life that had touched multiple generations in profoundly different ways.

Her journey from dancer to acclaimed actress to advocate created three distinct but interconnected legacies:

In entertainment, she left behind:
- Performances that defined comedy timing
- Characters that broke female stereotypes
- A model for career longevity and evolution
- Proof that supporting roles could become iconic

In advocacy, she provided:
- A template for celebrity health disclosure
- A voice that transformed MS awareness
- A bridge between entertainment and medical communities
- An example of turning personal challenges into public good

In personal inspiration, she demonstrated:

- How to face adversity with grace
- The power of humor in healing
- The importance of authenticity
- The art of reinvention at any age

The entertainment industry of 2024 barely resembled the one she entered as a young dancer in Elvis films. Yet her influence remained relevant because it wasn't just about performance technique – it was about approaching life with courage, humor, and unshakeable dignity.

As the tributes poured in, one theme became clear: Teri Garr's greatest performance wasn't in any film or television show. It was the example she set in how to dance through life's changes with grace, even when the music became challenging to hear.

Her final curtain call came on October 29, 2024, but the performance she began continues through:
- The artists she inspired
- The causes she championed
- The lives she touched
- The barriers she broke
- The paths she opened for others

In the end, Teri Garr's story transcended both entertainment and era. She showed us that life's greatest roles often come not from a script, but from how we face our most challenging moments. Her legacy dances on, teaching new generations that the most important performance is the one we give when the cameras stop rolling and real life begins.

Complete Filmography of Teri Garr

Early Dance Appearances (1963-1967)

- "Fun in Acapulco" (1963) - Dancer (Uncredited)
- "Viva Las Vegas" (1964) - Dancer (Uncredited)
- "Pajama Party" (1964) - Dancer
- "Roustabout" (1964) - Dancer (Uncredited)
- "The T.A.M.I. Show" (1964) - Dancer
- "Clambake" (1967) - Dancer (Uncredited)

Early Acting Roles (1968-1973)

- "Head" (1968) - Testy True (as Terry Garr)
- "Changes" (1969) - The Waitress
- "The Moonshine War" (1970) - Young Wife (as Terry Garr)

Breakthrough Period (1974-1979)

- "The Conversation" (1974) - Amy Fredericks
- "Young Frankenstein" (1974) - Inga
- "Won Ton Ton, the Dog Who Saved Hollywood" (1976) - Fluffy Peters
- "Oh, God!" (1977) - Bobbie Landers
- "Close Encounters of the Third Kind" (1977) - Ronnie Neary
- "The Black Stallion" (1979) - Mrs. Ramsey, Alec's Mother

Career Peak (1980-1985)

- "Tootsie" (1982) - Sandy Lester (Academy Award

nomination)

- "One from the Heart" (1982) - Frannie
- "The Sting II" (1983) - Loretta Gondorff
- "Mr. Mom" (1983) - Caroline Butler
- "After Hours" (1985) - Julie

Later Film Work (1986-2007)

- "Full Moon in Blue Water" (1988) - Louise Taylor
- "Let It Ride" (1989) - Pam
- "Mom and Dad Save the World" (1992) - Marge Nelson
- "Prêt-à-Porter" (1994) - Louise Hamilton
- "Dumb and Dumber" (1994) - Helen Swanson
- "Michael" (1996) - Judge Esther Newberg
- "Ghost World" (2001) - Maxine
- "Kabluey" (2007) - Suze (Final film role)

Notable Television Appearances

- "Batman" (1966) - Uncredited
- "The Andy Griffith Show" (1968)
- "MAS*H" (Multiple episodes)
- "McCloud" (Recurring role)
- "Saturday Night Live" (Host: 1980, 1983, 1985)
- "Friends" (1997-1998) - Phoebe Abbott Sr. (3 episodes)
- "Batman Beyond" (1999-2000) - Mary McGinnis (Voice)

This filmography represents Teri Garr's verified screen appearances, from her earliest uncredited dance roles to her final film performance, documenting a career spanning over four decades in Hollywood.

Television Appearances (Chronological Order)

1960s

- "Batman" (1966) - Uncredited appearance
- "The Andy Griffith Show" (1968) - Girl in Red Convertible
- "Star Trek" (1968) - Roberta Lincoln in "Assignment: Earth"
- "Mayberry R.F.D." (1968) - The Cashier
- "The Mothers-In-Law" (1969) - The Usherette
- "Room 222" (1969) - Marianne
- "It Takes a Thief" (1969) - Maggie Philbin (2 episodes)

1970s

- "McCloud" (1970-1975) - Sergeant Phyllis Norton/ Nora Mullins (6 episodes)
- "All in the Family" (1971) - Beverly
- "The Tonight Show Starring Johnny Carson" (1974) - Guest
- "The Sonny and Cher Comedy Hour" (1976) - Featured Performer

1980s

- "Saturday Night Live" (1980, 1983, 1985) - Host
- "The Muppet Show" (1982) - Guest
- "The Twilight Zone" (1985) - The Traveler

1990s

- "Good Advice" (1994) - Paige Turner (13 episodes)
- "Women of the House" (1995) - Sissy Emerson (12 episodes)
- "Frasier" (1995) - Nancy (Voice)
- "Friends" (1997-1998) - Phoebe Abbott (3 episodes)
- "ER" (1999) - Celinda Randlett
- "Batman Beyond" (1999-2000) - Mary McGinnis (Voice, 10 episodes)

2000s

- "King of the Hill" (2000) - Laney (Voice)
- "Strong Medicine" (2001) - Mimi Stark
- "The Young and the Restless" (2001) - Herself
- "Life with Bonnie" (2003) - Mrs. Abigail Portinbody
- "What's New, Scooby-Doo?" (2003) - Sandy Gordon (Voice)

Notable Talk Show Appearances

- Regular guest on "Late Night with David Letterman"
- Frequent appearances on "The Tonight Show Starring Johnny Carson"
- "Hollywood Squares" (2001-2002) - Panelist (25 episodes)
- "Jeopardy!" (1993-1998) - Celebrity Contestant (2 episodes)

This chronological listing represents Teri Garr's verified television appearances, showing her progression from bit parts to featured roles and guest appearances.

Awards and Nominations

Academy Awards

- 1983: Nominated - Best Supporting Actress for "Tootsie"

BAFTA Awards

- 1984: Nominated - Best Supporting Actress for "Tootsie"

Saturn Awards

- 1978: Nominated - Best Supporting Actress for "Close Encounters of the Third Kind"

National Society of Film Critics

- 1983: Third Place - Best Supporting Actress for "Tootsie"

CableACE Awards

- 1983: Nominated - Best Dramatic Actress for "Faerie Tale Theatre" (Episode: "The Tale of the Frog Prince")

National Board of Review

- 1994: Won - Best Acting Ensemble for "Prêt-à-Porter" (shared with ensemble cast)

Critical Recognition

- Pauline Kael, renowned film critic, called her "the funniest neurotic dizzy dame on the screen" (1982)
- Recognized as a "comedic legend" by industry peers
- Cited as an influence by performers including Jenna

Fischer and Tina Fey

Timeline of Major Life Events

1940s

- December 11, 1944: Born Terry Ann Garr in Lakewood, Ohio

1950s

- 1956: Father Eddie Garr dies of a heart attack when Teri is 11
- 1957: Family moves to San Fernando Valley, California

1960s

- Early 1960s: Begins training at San Francisco Ballet Company
- 1963-1967: Works as a dancer in Elvis Presley films
- 1968: First significant speaking role in "Star Trek" episode "Assignment: Earth"
- 1968: Appears in "Head" with The Monkees

1970s

- 1974: Breakthrough year with roles in "The Conversation" and "Young Frankenstein"
- 1977: Stars in "Close Encounters of the Third Kind"
- 1979: Appears in "The Black Stallion"

1980s

- 1982: Receives Academy Award nomination for "Tootsie"
- 1983: Stars in "Mr. Mom"
- 1985: Appears in Martin Scorsese's "After Hours"

- 1988: Arrested during nuclear weapons protest in Nevada

1990s

- 1993: Marries contractor John O'Neil
- 1993: Adopts daughter Molly
- 1996: Divorces John O'Neil
- 1997-1998: Recurring role on "Friends" as Phoebe's birth mother
- 1999: Receives MS diagnosis

2000s

- 2002: Publicly announces MS diagnosis on Larry King Live
- 2005: Publishes memoir "Speedbumps: Flooring It Through Hollywood"
- 2006: Survives brain aneurysm
- 2007: Final film roles in "Expired" and "Kabluey"

2020s

- October 29, 2024: Dies at age 79 from complications of multiple sclerosis, surrounded by family and friends

Notable Interview List

Television Interviews

"Late Night with David Letterman" (Multiple appearances 1982-1993)
- Including memorable pre-Oscar interview in 1983
- Known for witty banter and chemistry with Letterman

"Larry King Live" (2002)
- Historic interview where she publicly revealed her MS diagnosis

"Fresh Air with Terry Gross" (December 5, 2005)
- In-depth discussion about her memoir "Speedbumps"
- Detailed stories about "Young Frankenstein" and "Tootsie"

Print Media

Brain & Life Magazine (2005)
- Discussed managing MS: "Slowing down is so not in my nature, but I have to"
- Spoke about stress and anxiety affecting MS symptoms

People Magazine Interviews
- 2002: MS diagnosis revelation
- 2006: Memoir release coverage
- Multiple features throughout career

Notable Quotes from Interviews

- On her career: "I would like to play 'Norma Rae' and 'Sophie's Choice,' but I never got the chance"
- On MS diagnosis: "I was afraid that I wouldn't get work. People hear MS and think, 'Oh, my God, the person has two days to live'"
- On dealing with public perception: "You have to find your center and roll with the punches because that's a hard thing to do: to have people pity you"

Final Interviews

- Last major television appearance: "Law & Order: Special Victims Unit"
- Final public statements focused on MS advocacy and awareness
- Retired from acting and public appearances in 2011

This list represents verified interviews and public appearances, with particular focus on significant career moments and her advocacy work. Her final years were marked by fewer public appearances as she focused on health and family life.

Made in United States
Troutdale, OR
12/07/2024

26046724R00037